What Comes in a Shell?

Susan Canizares • Betsey Chessen

Scholastic Ltd

Design: MKR Design, Inc.

Photo Research: Barbara Scott

Endnotes: Susan Russell

Photographs: Cover: John Pontier/Animals, Animals.; p. 1: Nancy Rotenberg/Animals, Animals; p. 2: Jeff Foott/DRK Photo; p. 3: Andrew J. Martinez/Photo Researchers; p. 4: Gary Retherford/Photo Researchers; p. 5: DRK Photo; p. 6: Doug Wechsler/Animals, Animals; p. 7: Martyn Chillmaid; p. 8: Andrew J. Martinez/Photo Researchers; p. 9: Stephen G. Maka/DRK Photo; p. 10: John Pontier/Animals, Animals; p. 11: Neil G. McDaniel/ Photo Researchers; p. 12: Michael Furman/The Stock Market.

© 1998 by Scholastic Inc.

This edition © 2001 by Scholastic Ltd, Villiers House, Clarendon Avenue, Leamington Spa, Warwickshire CV32 5PR

British Library Cataloguing-in-Publication Data. A catalogue record for this book is available from the British Library.

ISBN 0-439-01946-X

Printed by Lynx Offset Ltd, Chalgrove.

1 2 3 4 5 6 7 8 9 0   1 2 3 4 5 6 7 8 9 0

What comes in a shell?

A crab comes in a shell.

A lobster does, too.

A prawn comes in a shell.

A barnacle does, too.

A scallop comes in a shell.

A snail does, too.

A mussel comes in a shell.

A clam does, too.

A conch comes in a shell.

An oyster comes in a shell...

sometimes with a pearl!

What Comes in a Shell?

When you go to the seashore, one of the first things you notice in the sand is seashells (page 1). They can be many different colours and shapes. Some look like fat spirals, some like twirling tops and others like little boats. Some even come as a matched pair hinged together like a door. These are called molluscs. There are other shells that are more complicated. They are exactly the shape of the animals inside, called arthropods. Shells are made when the fluid that is secreted by the sea creature hardens around it.

When crabs (page 2) grow bigger, their hard shells become too tight. When that happens, the shell splits open and the crab comes out covered in a very soft layer that hardens into its new, bigger shell. But while the shell is soft and papery, the crab is unprotected and easily eaten by other sea creatures – and humans, too! Lobsters (page 3) are another example of the arthropod family. Their shells are made of a substance called chitin.

The prawn (page 4) lives along the sea floor and eats the tiny organisms that make up plankton. Its shell becomes a bright orange when it is cooked for human food.

The barnacle (page 5) reminds us of a plant, but it's really an animal. It spends its life anchored to one spot, usually in an area where the tides can wash over it. When that happens, the barnacle opens the valves at the top of its shell and tiny feathery legs come out to sweep in the plankton that is their food. It closes its hard shell to protect it from the pounding waves.

A scallop (page 6) comes in two shells that are hinged together. These kinds of shells are called bivalves. When a scallop wants to move through the water, it flaps its shells together and the water that is squeezed out at the back propels it along. Snails (page 7) move along the bottom, carrying their shells with them. The soft part of their body that protrudes from the shell secretes a gooey slime that helps them slide more easily over the sand.

Baby mussels and clams (pages 8–9) begin life as eggs that hatch. Freshwater mussels stay in the mother's egg pouch until they have very tiny shells. Then, when a fish passes close by, the mussels clamp on and burrow into its tissue, which keeps them nourished. In a couple of weeks, they emerge to sink to the bottom of the stream, where they grow the shell of adult mussels. Clams are found burrowed into the sand. They keep their strong shells locked tightly together for protection from predators.

The shell of the conch (page 10) grows a little at a time, spiralling outwards as the animal inside gets bigger and needs more space. To eat, the conch extends a long, soft footlike part of its body into the shells of other molluses. The edge of the small mouth can cut off bits of meat while the tongue-like part that is covered with tiny teeth can grind it down.

Oysters (page 11) glue themselves to rocky places at the bottom of the sea and make very thick shells with a special fluid. They get food by siphoning the plankton-rich water into their two shells.

If a tiny pebble gets inside the oyster's shell (page 12), it uses its shell-building fluid to surround the pebble. This builds up, layer by layer, until a pearl is formed.